SLEEP

SLEEP

(Fifteen Poems)

by

Peter W. Katsirubas

AEOLUS PRESS

Falls Church, VA

ISBN 0-9616166-0-1

Printed in the United States of America

CONTENTS

SLEEP

Sleep is a pool of darkness,
effused from the well of solace;

Sleep is a restless blessing
riding the finger tips of the wind;

Sleep is a medicinal refuge;
Sleep is the suppliant's peace;

for every journey there is a fate,
a guide to each conclusion;

Sleep,
be benumbed,
journey with me.

EVOLUTION

1

A time spirals past all men
when illusion is the essence of being,
when it seems someone, somewhere
               possesses an answer.

There escaped a time
when the earth was a rain forest to be raped,
when the river Omo licked life into arboreal man
            as if to say:

            "Flow free.
            come down from your branches,
            leave the lemurs and follow me."

Step
     by step
         the Javanese
             cannibal recoiled
                  into his cave;

       there could he dwell
    secure in the knowledge that
       fire would keep
            beasts off his throat,

  till the embers cooled,
  till the smoked dispersed..

      Till the embers ash
  a mind can belong to itself,
       plotting plots of dreams, dreaming
           of succulent fruits, of maidens.

  How I will fortify my boundaries,
  till the ashes cool
        when the rains come.

3

　. . . dots
　becoming---------------
　lines becoming men

The old Chinaman would learn,
lapping rice from an onyx bowl
in the jade valley of the turquoise stream,
scorning the shade of the bodhi tree
that grew in the three fields of cinnabar.

Cooled by peacock feather fans,
pondering the wisdom of oracular bones,
　　　　　　his time would come;
　　　　　　he would depart
　　　　　　from the future
　　　　　　to the past.

A minor cataclysm,
nothing more or less
than a chronic evolution of letters:

pneumonoultramicroscopicsilicovolcanokoniosis

CLOUDS

Clouds

---> direction

------------------->

---> motion

---------------------------> circular ----------------
)
            (--
             \----------------> elusive freedom

--------------------------->

---------------------------> designs

                    --> voices in form

------------> escape

---> destiny

d
  i
    s
      s
        o
         l
           v
             e
              d

OUTSIDERS' DAYS

1

Mornings are born in the night,
  in a warm bed, by a cold street,
  in the secrets of a subconscious mind at peril in the dark;
                floundering
          in the infinite,
            the grotesque,
          in the colorless black,
            the void,
 in the body
  at the point where all the veins find meaning,
  in the mind where the webs of blood confront the unknown.

It is the dawn of the Day of Ascension.
The graceless ghosts of images have been conjured,
their knucklebones bared from torn ulcerated fists
dripping tissues of flesh on the rusted bars through
                  which they escaped;
       taking shape,
       taking substance,
       taking substance from their creator;
            draining him,
   coming, the disease of being to destroy their god.

The cancerous forms are fused into one and it comes.
The suffocating force of past experiences
drawn from the welled up waters of dreams,
undiluted, pure in essence, potent, is coming closer
                 coming with intent.

2

I have been,
is that concise?
A whole,
A unit,
     One.
Then re-stamped, re-pressed,
re-formed into a distorted figure.

I am not what I am,
You are not what you are.

We have been broiled on hot asphalt at high noon together,
                we have glared in the sun,
we have been tread upon by corporations and tires of progress.

We have been pried from our shelters,
crowbars have stolen us like nails from over ripened crates.

We have been exposed like leafless trees in winter,
snow melting on us in the afternoon rays
to liquefy in order
to freeze to ice tonight.

3

Afternoons of infinite oblivion;

sipping tea,
stirring winds and banners of bamboo,
dealing rubbers,

drinking Scotch,
filling orders and bottomless cabinets,
building formulas.

It was a day ideal for a wake. It was a month that only the wind attended.
The brittle carcass of a leaf fluttered like the wings of a hummingbird.
No witches emerged in primeval dress to cackle their accomplishments.
No gods or devils clamored into combat for the soul of the unseen
                that clung like steel in desperation,
                            in degradation,
            that fell still sucking moisture,

                    that landed
                split and naked
        to the sun that gifted the green and infused the palsying brown
                at no extra expense.

4

The time has come for moronic men.
Like insects without minds hovering a torpid marsh,
    not knowing what they must do,
            unable to realize what they have done,
            they run.

Their metal cubes contain them,
they trail like segments of a snake,
        winding,
        curving,
        joining like socketed vertebrae;

      searching for the appeasement
they bought at the cost of renouncing it;

      peering through the eyes
of a multiheaded monster
with all members connected to one Gargantuan body.

It has no genitals,
It has no uterus,
    they have been cut off, cut out.
    Its day has come,
    and by coming has consumed all mercy.

5

This evening is our evening.
This evening our American Evangelist
called for the castration of rapists.

> Hallowed be his name.
> May his kingdom come.
> May the ignorant rule, completely.

He knows the subtleties of the Good Book,
he knows the sledge weight of its ambiguities,
may his demonic calling manifest its results upon us.

We have sweated enough today, it is time for our dinner.
We have given what we have, a portion of our One Life.
They have taken what is ours, a portion of our One Life
while procuring more malevolent interest rates.

> May their kingdom come, also.

All is gone from us,
but we exist.

Because we hope,
we struggle.
Because we struggle
like sea urchins with their spine needles snapped,
at odds in our own element,
we fail.
They succeed.

> But if we die
> they perish with us.

6

What narcotic has addicted us
to these tubercular days?
What hopeless hope?

Expectancy? Anticipation?

Are those our new gods?
Our charcoal born of frail ash?
The fire leaves no remains.

The good is better than the bad,
but even in the good
futility bares her rabid jaws.

No soothing hand is extended
to relieve the isolated souls.

So their bottles are uncorked,
   their cigarettes rolled,
   their syringes boiled,

and a generation's despair is defeated, but not destroyed.
              It regroups
              to return

              And it will,
              and it does,
              amen.

7

The night has returned with full intensity.
Decisions must be made.
Important matters cannot be put off.

The madman, the Anglophile,
the gas drunk woman rot.

Those without voices are permitted to speak.
Those without ears are permitted to hear.

While they languish gutted and hung in suspended animation
   the atmosphere of my room thickens and congeals.

My blood has turned one hundred proof,
my lungs are filled with smoke.

I perceive levels of insight
and at their peak
the white clad curator by his antiseptic door.

                    Though I cannot speak,
                    and must read his lips,
                        I understand
                        he calls;

                        good-bye.

GREEN TREES

.green trees blown bare
at the coldest time, no screams of pain
or for relief just trembless bark
about the house like a wreath

without birds, about the cold bleeding
bricks surrounding sounds of supper and
plastic plates and white drawn faces
cold at the coldest timE

THE SETTING SUN

The sun is setting,
the pale pulp of light is fading
behind the bud laden branches of trees;
the green lawn is becoming cold and hard,
the birds have deserted us.

The sun is setting in the wailing wind,
we must adjust to the absence of the light,
we must find patience for the night,
the sun is setting fast.

Dark haired Kathy was nineteen,
what did she know of life?
That death is a reality?
Kathy is dead,
and the sun is setting.

APATHY

No!

In the dead time of night.
In the dead of the deadest night
the tide flows
upon the beach.

During the longest night of the year,
During the coldest night of the year,
the star frozen Sagittarian night of the year
the tide flows
ice cubes in the sand.

Only a siren can move the living dead
        that night of the year,
Only a siren can move them
        during the deadest night of the year,
        during the night of nights
        while the tide flows.
Only a siren will move them,
        if they are able to move at all.

PERSIAN TRILOGY

1. Desire

2. Masnevi

3. Persian's Lament

DESIRE

Desire is a throb at the center of the universe,
                an ache,
                a tension.

Oscillating planets is one wave of its satisfaction,
                a spasm,
                electricity.

It permeates all matter, it is the soul of all things,
                wind driven sand,
                rain inspired thought.

The sensual renewal of life penetrates the rose garden
whispering, "I breathe," in the lilac attar of Jasmine.

MASNEVI

Once sight alone of her unclad shoulder
could arouse the passions of her lover.
Now her embrace is a cold reunion,
her kiss on my lips, suffocation.

PERSIAN'S LAMENT

I might as well be living
in the outlands, the badlands,
the wasteland
watching the sun shrivel and segment
the earth.

It was Iceland
killed the Dinosaur,
woke the creatures senseless in limbo
on the ocean bed,
put the mad deception into their heads
that living was more than just survival.

ECCE HOMO

. . . asked who he was
Buddha replied, "I am awake."

Jesus Christ
man,
in Allah's name
have you any idea what that meant Lao?

It wasn't anything, but
it ain't nothing either.

I know, being both the rock that Sisyphus must balance
and being Sisyphus himself.

Bared. Compulsive. Contradictory.

I am . . .
I . . .

CIVILIZATION

1

I jumped ship at Corcyra.
I told my captain the golden fleece was his
                              and all its misery;
I told my captain his betrothed was a bitch
                              that she cast spells on me,
disturbed the serenity of my sea blown dreams,
                              bewitched me with her siren's song.

I had been a parasite at my father's table too long,
too long infected with the spirit of the muse,
a tormented trophy of Erato's abuse,
                              mercifully, I fled.

My odyssey began without regrets,
it was time I ceased to be misled,
one dead end is as bitter as another.

The ibis shares no secrets,
 wind over marsh plants does not whisper to lovers;
 Khepera is incapable of self-regeneration,
 the Nile is sacred though not a woman.

Words do not trip off the lips of mummified kings,
their sarcophagi are sepulchered where no bird sings.
Sand consumes all the imprints of man,
the white caps of the sea become the clouds of the sky
for men borne beyond the reason why.

2

War is the ingenuous art
of political usurpation,
lethal as a game of chess.

A prime minister dispatched to subvert a king,
a knight to impede the progress of a bishop,
a game of consequences.

The great Raja in exile, in a mango grove
in littoral Malaya, visited by Lord Krsna,
became an initiate and player.

Guided by the dictates of his Lord,
espousing the esoteric principles of this art form,
he enlisted me in his jihad with the noble rank of pawn.

A soldier's life
is a miserable lot when
dying is for other men's glories.

Routed in the ambush neath the Carchamian walls,
broken in the gambit on the Charonean Plains,
incinerated in the rain forests of Indo-China,
abandoned on the cavernous Afghani slopes, no more.

War is the pleasurable pastime of the immortal gods.
I will bleed no more for generals nor their mortal ministers,
nor raze Sicilian defenses for the mating of corporate marionettes.
I un-holster my Magnum for freedom alone, and then, only my own.

3

Where once the elements of time and space propitiously conjoined, in Bagdad, under
the enlightened eye of benevolent Al Monsour, where
nights were never long enough, there lived a moment in which to spend one's youth.

Those who never had a youth, and there have been many such half-lived creatures
hording a vitality which nature provides but one season for spending,
could never fathom how Ali, the procurer, and I mainlined life through open veins.

Desrter from all common causes, anarchist, denouncer of the good life
according to Madison Avenue and social humanism,
I wallowed in my nympholeptic dreams of paradise tasted on this earth.

Sleeping through the heat of the day, stirring with the orange breeze of sunset,
sipping chamomile tea, supping on Turkish cannabis delights, I, sultan
of the Alhambra, summoned the moist lips of my night's desire with a pomegranate.

Ali supplied the maidens for my fountain, ivory women from the fjords of ice,
almond-eyed dancers with delicate limbs, a princess
of Mali black in her beauty, dark haired girls with firm, inviting bellies.

Dry Cyprian wine, golden white in its intensity, wrapped in the undefiled snows
of Mount Meru, warmed the sweet hunger of our passions.
I fell into welcome embraces, was coaxed through the humid forests of love.

Sappho and Khayyam were my poets, Ovid and Vatsyayana my teachers, Diogenes
my conscience, and the intellectual's philodoxical quagmire
was exorcised by the blessings of the moment, the sighs of an actual *occasion.*

4

He jumped ship at Corcyra,
abandoned his post dishonorably.
He has succumbed to the lethargic death throes
of civilization's last delirium, its final delusion.
An epicurean unaware of the virtues of Epicurus,
he is a nihilistic absurdity
flouting his alienation like a badge of honor.

He talks only to hear himself think,
his soul has no concept of being.
He is a creature neither alive nor dead
living in the demi-monde of twilight and shadows.
Ignoring is his article of faith, he is insensate
to the venal sanctity of business
or religion, the only civilized paths to salvation.

A malevolent pariah
opposed to the Puritan ethic,
more venomous than Medusa's vile blood,
wasting a lifetime of cost ineffective days
vainly pursuing the uncharted course of his dreams,
a plague to be exterminated,
society decries the unlawfulness of his existence.

5

I have observed the esurient masses   crouched gape-mouthed in
doorways   I have wandered among them   been there   palms up   on
the razor's edge of fear   a Hamlet pondering the threshold of my
tolerance

old women   callous-kneed   praying matises at rosewood altars
     pleading for the survival of their offspring   material recognition of
their common humanity   liberation from the Aztec   the messiah
came   gentile Cortez   Nero for Stalin   and he tore out their tongues

during the seduction of my generation   the war for beads of sugar
     an invitation to the land of milk and honey   paradise within a world
of diminishing resources   I cast myself into the chaotic abyss
anchorless on etesian winds   I struggled to find order and reason

I could have slaughtered infants   risen to the rulership of nations
     established a monopoly in Nippon   fulfilled the prophesies of socio-
biologists   ignored the Sphinx   Delphic truth: to be alive is to live in
an ocean of the senses   which feed our emotions determining our
thoughts

life is not empirical data   technologically ensiled   nor the world as
my idea or will   life is my dream   as dreams are the substance of
humanity   the only obstacle to holocaustic insanity

THE OCEAN

A vision of the ocean
recurs in my thoughts;
a fog lifts and it is there,
the view aerial,
the movement incessant.

A patch of melting snow
becomes the parted fog,
the sun an unrefracted fleck of gold
upon its surface swell.

The image is immutable
yet the ocean is inconstant,
both violent and serene,
its nature ever present
and ever unrevealed,
an enigmatic reflection
of an involuted thought.

A REPORT OF SUICIDE

Lettuce should be torn, never cut.

And on his thirty-sixth birthday
he tore his life from its connection with time,
the only umbilical cord of consequence.

If only he had turned about once more.
Pressing his eyelids, blackening his sight,
If only he had ceased to think, once more.

Was it the absurdity of life that overwhelmed him,
the need to chart its trackless wastes
within the map that was his soul?

If only he had found a guidepost,
one oasis in that waterless land,
if only he had reached out, just once more.

SLEEP

You have been taken from me.
The emptiness of my existence
        was not profound enough.
        Your blood was needed
        to complete the void.
If I had faith in death
I would follow you today.

But in death there are no dreams,
so I must tolerate senseless life
to await the catharsis of sleep.

For only in the dreams of sleep
might we, in dimensionless space, meet.
        And I will touch your forehead,
        and I will nourish you,
        ask about your wanderings,
and, till wakened, watch
over you while you sleep.

About the author

P. W. Katsirubas is an American novelist, poet and screenwriter. Born on Guam, he has lived in Greece, Pakistan and Iran, and attended American, Catholic and Georgetown Universities in Washington D. C. He has published a book of poetry entitled Sleep (Fifteen Poems). The novels, Santorini (with an Aegean setting) and The Idle Pursuit of Pleasure (set in 1925 Paris), Paris and Helen of Troy, as well as a children's mythology book The Legend of King Minos are available as Kindle e-books as well as paperback.

Other books by Peter W. Katsirubas

Santorini (a novel)

The Idle Pursuit of Pleasure

Paris and Helen of Troy

The Legend of King Minos (Greek Mythology for young readers)